Embrace what you don't know, especially in the beginning, because what you don't know can become your greatest asset. It ensures that you will absolutely be doing things differently from everybody else.

Sara Blakely

Acclaim

"Writing a proper business plan is one of those things that sounds quite simple initially, but becomes rather challenging eventually. Tiffany has done a great service both to students and instructors by putting all the necessary components in an easy-to-understand format, enabling all to have a clear path to follow that will lead to a complete and presentable business plan."

Alp Ozaman, Regional Marketing Manager, Turkish Airlines, New York

"Refreshingly accessible, avoiding 'corporatese' and business jargon, this is a workbook that really works. With the detail we need and none we don't, Johnson's book takes us step-by-step through the though processes and the execution to deliver first-class business plans. I'll be recommending the book to several people I know will be grateful — and using it myself."

Angus McCallum, Managing Principal, Valent Strategic Communications

"Genius Ideas transforms the daunting exercise of business planning into an actionable process. A blend of reflection, strategic thinking and interactivity empowers everyone to navigate the path to entrepreneurship with confidence."

Daniela Molta, Assistant Professor, Advertising,
S.I. Newhouse School of Public Communications

"An enriching, smart, and fun way to sink your teeth into the world of entrepreneurship with this engaging and practical Business Planning Workbook. Tiffany takes her own learnings in business and translates it for those looking for a way in without it feeling too daunting."

Emma Chiu, Global Director, VML Intelligence

Acclaim

"With 'Genius Ideas,' Tiffany masterfully breaks down intricate work into fundamental components, demystifying and simplifying the process of developing a comprehensive business plan. This workbook guides entrepreneurs through critical steps in a fun and approachable manner, resulting in a clear and insightful roadmap to launching their business."

Cathy Gribble, Marketing Analyst Professional

■■■■■■■■■■■■■■■■■■■■■■

"A great resource for entrepreneurs – it perfectly encapsulates the steps in writing and perfecting a business plan. Easy to understand and easy to use."

David Vinjamuri, Associate Professor of Marketing (adj.), New York University
Author of "Accidental Branding: How Ordinary People Build Extraordinary Brands" (Wiley, 2008)

■■■■■■■■■■■■■■■■■■■■■■

"This book is absolutely essential for anyone starting a business, or studying startups. Starting a business can be daunting, this book gives you a framework to turn your dreams into ideas, your ideas into plans, and your plans into actions. It will save you time, money and heartache. Do not start a new endeavor without working through this book first."

Chris Miller, People Manager, Malone Solutions

■■■■■■■■■■■■■■■■■■■■■■

"Tiffany has created an excellent guide that breaks down the process in a way that is organized, easy to follow, and even fun. By providing examples and words of wisdom alongside step-by-step sections, this book makes business planning understandable and approachable for students and new entrepreneurs alike. I am happy to offer my endorsement of this useful resource that can support both academic and real-world applications for developing ideas into actionable plans."

Shahrukh Bari, Ad Tech Manager

Genius Ideas

Business Plan Workbook

Your Roadmap to Success

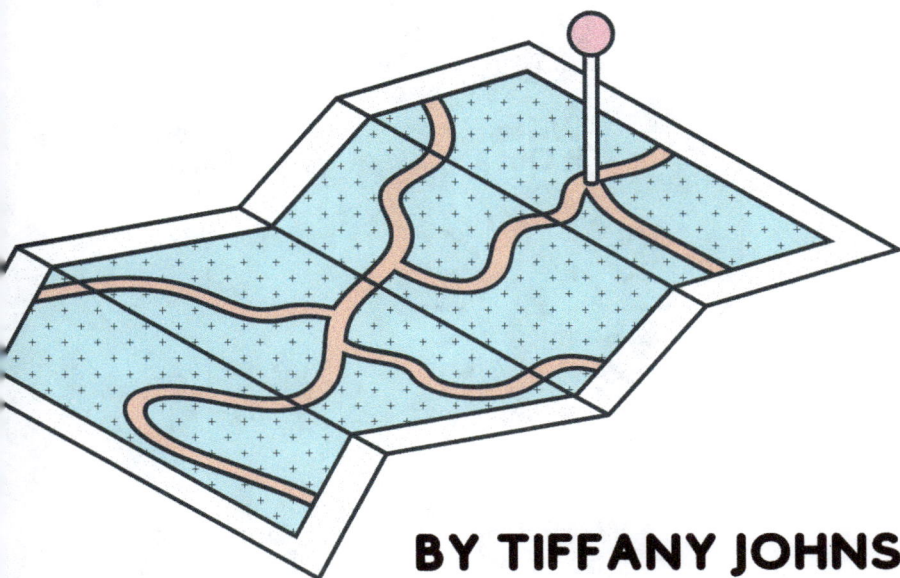

BY TIFFANY JOHNSON

Welcome

This is your business plan workbook. It's meant to be written in, torn up, thrown across the room, taped up, repaired, cried on and shared.

This is your journey, your path to success, and only you can define what success means to you.

Don't stop now—turn the page and get started on your dream!

Icon Reference Guide

Learning Moment

Write It Out

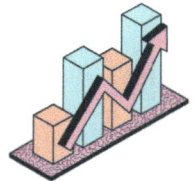

Research Needed

Friendly Feedback

Workshop Session

Unplug and Take a Break

Business Plan Workbook

Table of Contents

Business Plan Workbook

Icon Definitions

Learning Moment

Learning Moments are pages meant for you to read, learn from and reflect on before starting on the section. They provide information and instructions to complete sections in the workbook.

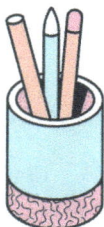

Write It Out

Write It Out means this is a page for you to answer questions posed by writing things down. This will give you an opportunity to stop and think about what you're doing along with keeping a record of information to help you on your business plan journey.

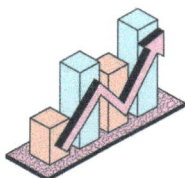

Research Needed

Research Needed pages indicate where you need to find more information about your business. There are plenty of areas to keep learning about your business, and research plays an important part.

Business Plan Workbook

Icon Definitions

Friendly Feedback

Having trusted friends and colleagues is important to success, so the Friendly Feedback sections help you remember the importance of collaboration and encourage you to seek outside thoughts. Just remember to listen and filter for what makes sense for you and your business.

Workshop Session

Workshop Session pages are meant to be inspirational, fun activities that will help you better define aspects of your business plan. Workshops can be done individually or with colleagues.

Unplug and Take a Break

Unplug and Take a Break sections remind you that your best work is sometimes done while you're not at work. There is a life outside of work, and it can be beneficial to step away and enjoy that life in between completing sections of the workbook.

Stop Dreaming, Start Doing

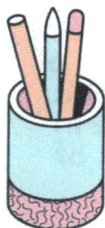

My Executive Pitch

What is an executive pitch?

An executive pitch is how you explain your business idea in one minute or less. It is also referred to as an elevator pitch.

Picture this: you step onto an elevator with the one person who would fund your business, and you have about 10 floors to sell your genius idea!

Your executive pitch should be 2–3 sentences that explain your idea and why we should care. You'll want to include the problem you solve and how you solve it.

Use the next few pages to scribble and ideate. Don't worry about getting your executive pitch perfect this time around—the important first step is that you get your initial business idea on paper!

Executive Pitch Checklist

- ☐ **Problem Statement**
- ☐ **Business Idea**
- ☐ **Unique Solution**
- ☐ **Heart!** ♥

Skills Assessment

You're a talented, skilled individual with an amazing business idea. But you can't do it all!

Now is the time to assess your strengths and skills. Doing this will give you insight into who you are, your values, your strengths and how you interact with others. Learning about yourself during the early stages of your business planning will help you. It will impact how you run your business, how to align your business to long-standing values and how you best work with others. Additionally, you can identify gaps in your skills, knowledge and even beliefs and attitudes.

Identifying these gaps will help you understand where to best use your time for the business, what you need to learn and who you need to hire.

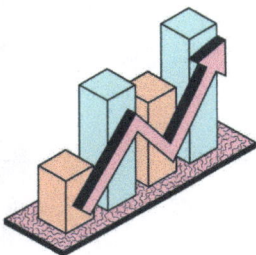

Options to take skills and personality assessments online:

Personality Type Finder – Truity.com
Values – Personalvalu.es
Principles – Principlesyou.com

Who are you?

I took this assessment: _____

Here is what I learned about myself (results):

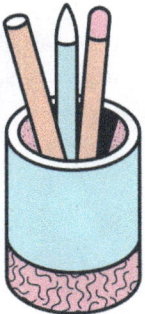

What matters to you?

A list of my values (what is most important):

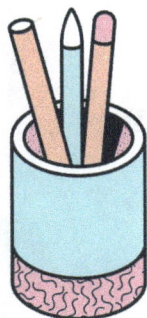

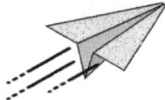

How do you work with others?

I am most compatible with people who:

I am least compatible with people who:

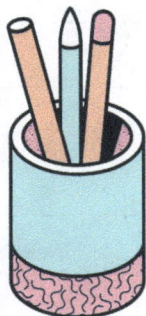

What are your skills?

I am strongest at:

I could use help with:

Who knows you best? Now is a great time to reach out and get some friendly feedback on how your friends and family perceive your strengths and areas where you might need help.

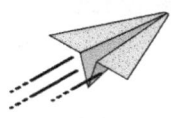

Who do you need to hire?

I need people with these personalities:

I need people with these skills:

Unplug and Take a Break

You've done a lot of work understanding who you are, so you're prepared to be in the best place to start your business and know who you need to hire. Next up is the executive summary, where you'll take on the heavy lifting of researching and proving out your idea.

But first, take a break, unplug from your digital devices, let your mind roam, and have fun! A well-rested, happy mind will put you in a better place to tackle the next stages.

A big business starts small.

Richard Branson

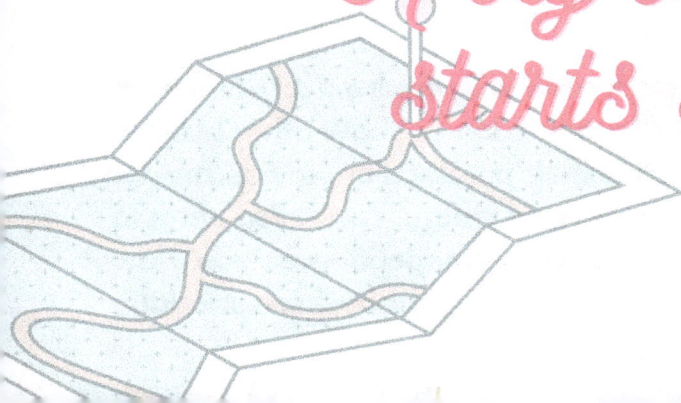

Executive Summary

An executive summary is a short, well-researched overview of your business idea.

This is a first pass at the executive summary, so it doesn't have to be perfect. It is more important that you spend the time researching and thoughtfully considering how your business is solving a marketplace challenge and how you differ from your competitors. This section will give you initial goals and guidelines to help you complete the next sections of the journal.

At the end of the journal, you'll rewrite the executive summary, using the information you collected throughout your research and learnings in this and other sections. This will ensure your executive summary is refined, using your new knowledge, to present to people who might fund your business or support it in other ways.

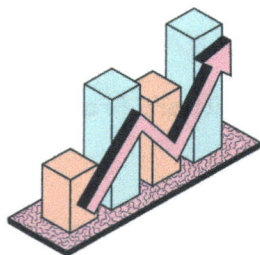

This section will require a lot of research! You'll want to look at how other businesses define their products or service, mission, values and vision. You'll also want to research your competition, so you'll know what makes your business special.

The Executive Summary Contains:

- **Brief Description of Your Product or Service**
  - 1–2 sentences clearly describing your offering

- **Statement of Marketplace Need**
  - 1–2 sentences stating the problem you see in the market

- **How Your Business Solves the Marketplace Need**
  - A few short sentences on how your product or service solves the problem you see in the marketplace, including the benefit to your customers

- **Competitors in the Market**
  - Research a few competitors to see how they are addressing the marketplace need you identified (you'll dig deeper into competition later!)

- **Unique Selling Proposition**
  - How are you different from your competitors? What makes your business solution the best for the marketplace need?

  - **Mission Statement**
    - Why do you exist? What is your overall goal and purpose?

  - **Business Values**
    - Beliefs, philosophies, and principles that drive your business, what matters to your business and how you present to your customers

  - **Business Vision**
    - Where your company will be in the future. Align this to your business mission, goals and values

How would you describe your product or service?

What is the marketplace need that aligns to your business?

How does your business solve the marketplace need?

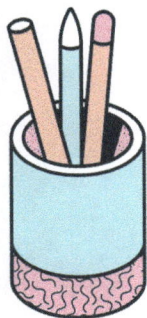

Who are your competitors?

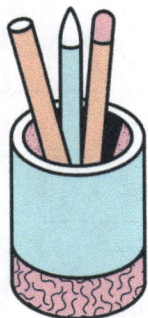

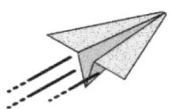

What makes you special?
How is your business different?

What is your company's motivation? Why does solving the marketplace need matter to you and your company?

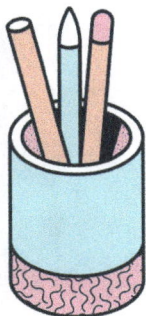

Mission Statement

Why do you exist? What is your purpose?

Business Values

Beliefs, philosophies, and principles that drive your business - what matters to your business? How do you want your customers to see you?

Business Vision

Where will your company be in the future?
Pro Tip - Align to your mission, goals and values

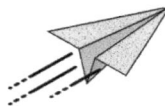

Organizational Plan

An organizational plan is where you map out the structure of your business, choose your team and start to think about finances.

You'll have to learn how to determine how much to charge for your product, how to charge for it, how to staff your business, how to do a deep dive into your competitors, and how to conduct a SWOT (strengths, weaknesses, opportunities, threats) analysis.

- **Business Model** – Your method of doing business and generating revenue. How are you going to charge for your product or service? How do customers purchase your product or service?
- **Strategy** – Short- and long-term objectives and how you plan to achieve them.

- **Staffing Needs & Plan** – You already know the kinds of people you need to hire. Now let's focus on the skills you need to run your business.
- **Competitors** – Who are your primary competitors? How are they doing business? What do they charge?
- **SWOT Analysis** – An analysis of your business's strengths, weaknesses, opportunities and threats compared to your competitors and what's happening in the marketplace right now. It allows you to identify areas to emphasize, areas to focus on and areas of need.

Unplug and Take a Break

Organizational plans are research-heavy and intensive work. You've made it through the first parts of your business planning, so before you tackle the next section, it's a good idea to take a break.

Unplug from your digital devices, go outside or to another room, read a book you enjoy or meditate. Breaks can take many forms. The point is to let your mind rest and contemplate what's next.

The most important investment you can make is in yourself.

Warren Buffett

Business Model

I plan to generate revenue by (selling online, opening a retail store, offering a service, etc.):

What amount will I charge for products or services?

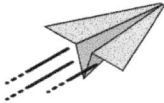

Strategy – What are your short- and long-term objectives?

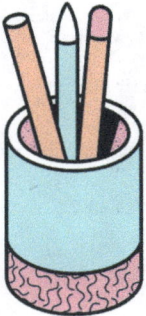

How do you plan to achieve the objectives you set?

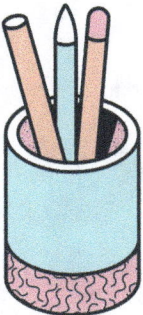

Staffing Needs

I need the following people to run my business:

How much do you plan to pay for staff or needed services?

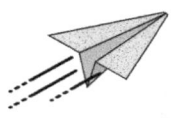

Staffing Plan – Who is responsible for what work, and how should the staff be structured?

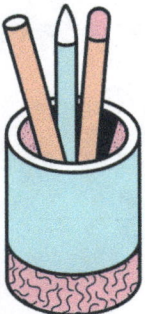

Competitors – Add 3 –5 of your top business competitors:

1.

2.

3.

4.

5.

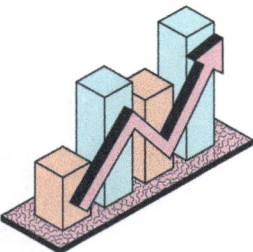

Competitive Depth

You've listed your competitors, but the work isn't finished. The more you know about your competition, the better you'll understand how you can differentiate from them. This section is about competitive depth, which will give you useful information that will help in your planning—you'll either find what makes you truly different from your competitors or you'll find ways to partner with them to make your offering stronger.

- **Website** – List the website address and what you noticed on the site about their use of design, colors and user experience.
- **Social Media Accounts** – What social media are they using, and how are they using it? What's good or bad?
- **Description of Product Service or Offering** – Describe the main product or offering that competes with yours. Be strategic in your description and research, so you know how your business is different or better.
- **How much do they charge?** Can you compete on price? Or do you need to compete on quality or other services?
- **What is their business model?** Do you know how you're planning to make money? Is it the same or different from your business model?

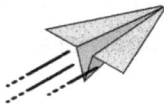

Competitor Name:

Website:

Social media accounts:

Description of product or service offering:

How much do they charge?

What is their business model?

Competitor Name:

Website:

Social media accounts:

Description of product or service offering:

How much do they charge?

What is their business model?

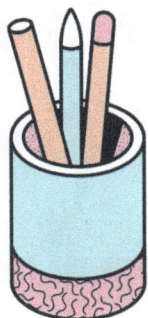

Competitor Name:

Website:

Social media accounts:

Description of product or service offering:

How much do they charge?

What is their business model?

Competitor Name:

Website:

Social media accounts:

Description of product or service offering:

How much do they charge?

What is their business model?

Competitor Name:

Website:

Social media accounts:

Description of product or service offering:

How much do they charge?

What is their business model?

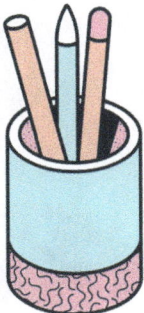

Say It Again – Why is your product or service better?

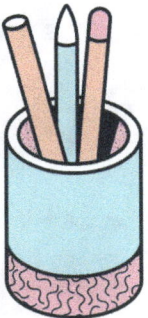

Unplug and Take a Break

Competition is fierce, but so are you! Take a break before you tackle the next section. Go for a walk, find a friend, read a book... Whatever you do, remind yourself that you are capable and you can be successful—one day at a time.

> Dreams do not come true just because you dream them. It's hard work that makes things happen. It's hard work that creates change.

Shonda Rhimes

What Is a SWOT Analysis?

SWOT (Strengths, Weaknesses, Opportunities, Threats) is an analysis of what's best in your business, where you need to make things better, market opportunities and areas that could be problematic for your business.

1. Grab a bunch of sticky notes and some colorful markers, then find a wall you can use.
2. Don't overthink—write what first comes to mind when you think about the categories.
   a. Strengths – What is your competitive advantage? What makes you stand out?
   b. Weaknesses – Where are your gaps? Where do your competitors excel and you don't yet?
   c. Opportunities – Where can you grow in the future? How can you get your start and keep expanding?
   d. Threats – What could cause you to falter or fail? What do you need to watch out for?
3. Take 5 minutes for each category and write everything that comes to mind.
4. Place them on the wall under a heading for each category.
5. Take a break—overnight or for at least an hour.
6. Come back, narrow down the most important items and write them on the pages below.

Friendly Feedback

Tackling a SWOT analysis for your business takes deep insight and thought. You need to know your business well. More importantly, you need a fresh perspective. Gather your closest friends and colleagues, and ask them about the strengths and weaknesses of your business ideas. Then, if they are willing, ask them how they see your opportunities and biggest threats. Record the best thoughts you collected on the following pages.

The key to success is to do the common things uncommonly well.

Oprah Winfrey

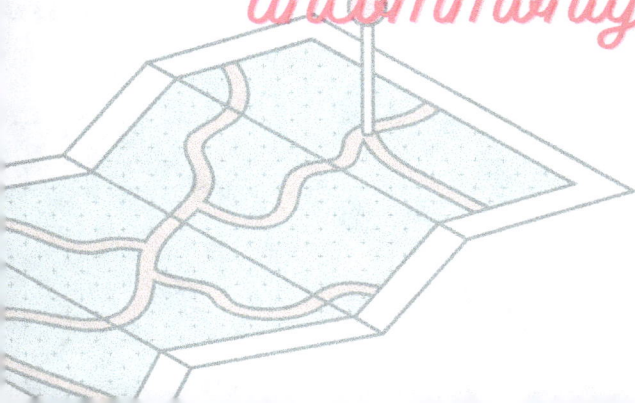

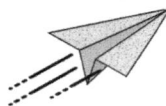

Strengths

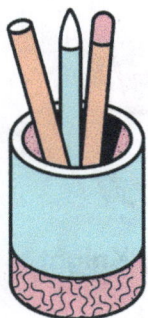

" *I don't believe in luck,*
I believe in preparation.

Bobby Knight

Weaknesses

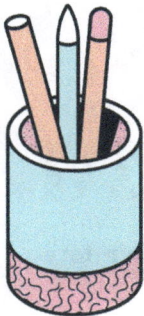

> I couldn't wait for success,
> so I went ahead without it.

Jonathan Winters

Opportunities

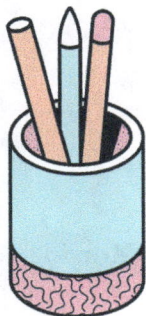

> One way to keep momentum going is to have constantly greater goals.
>
> **Michael Korda**

Threats

Entrepreneurs understand there is little difference between obstacle and opportunity.

Victor Kiam

SWOT Mapping

Put Your Top Inputs Here

Strengths

Weaknesses

Opportunities

Threats

Unplug and Take a Break

Up next is the marketing plan! It's a large portion of work, and you'll need to have a clear head to research your market, identify target audiences and trends, and make decisions about how you want to tell people about your business. Take this as an opportunity to pause and consider how far you've come before you proceed!

> Don't ever make decisions based on fear. Make decisions based on hope and possibility.

Michelle Obama

Marketing Plan

A good marketing plan will guide your introduction to the world—and to your key consumers!

This plan will be comprehensive, so you will know your ideal customer and strategically develop a plan to reach them. This will keep you focused on where to best spend your time and money. There are several elements to include in your plan.

- **Target Market** – The market you want to focus on, your ideal customer with attitudes and behaviors that matter to your business, and where you can reach customers.
- **Industry Trends** – What is popular right now that could impact your business for better or worse?
- **Advertising Plan** – Where do you reach your ideal consumer? What kind of money do you want to set aside for advertising costs?

- **Social Media Strategy** – What platforms will have the biggest impact?
- **Creative & Content** – Based on your advertising and social media strategy plans, what kind of content and creative do you need to consider? Should you hire someone to help with this?
- **Public Relations (PR) Plan** – Outreach or earned media that promotes awareness of your business.

Friendly Feedback

In the end, businesses are about people. As you consider your target market, go to your trusted friends and colleagues, describe your business idea to them and ask them: Who do you think would be most interested in this? Write the best thoughts here:

What helps people, helps business.

Leo Burnett

What is a target market?

Your target market is the portion of a population that is most likely to purchase your product or service.

It's important to define your target market and your ideal customer so you can focus your marketing, advertising, creative and content to fit their needs. Doing this will help you stay focused and save money on marketing or media investment. You'll also know when to say no to content, creative or advertising that won't have meaning for your customers.

Your target market should be narrow and easy to sell to (think about why they need your business!). This will help you gain traction and generate revenue, from which you will continue to grow.

A target market can include demographics, which indicate basics about your target markets (e.g., household income, number of kids, marital status, gender, location, etc.).

Demographics are somewhat outdated in today's market and should only be applied if it makes sense for your business. The real focus is on your consumer's attitudes and behaviors— How do they feel about the issue you're solving? What other products do they consume? How do they interact with your product or service? Where do they hear your message—on social, TV, on the drive, radio, online? Are they introverts, extroverts, ambiverts? Be specific, build your target market and then define your ideal customer!

Target Market Research

Behaviors & Attitudes – Who is most likely going to purchase your product or service?

Demographics (Optional)

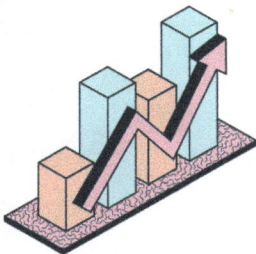

Target Market Research

Where are you most likely to find your consumer? Are they online or on social platforms? Do they read magazines or visit certain websites?

Create your list here:

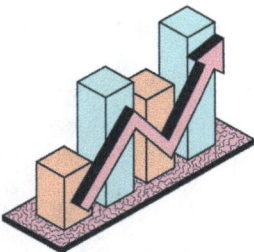

How would you define your ideal customer?

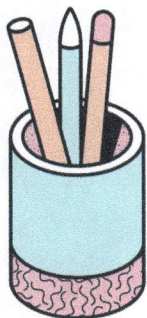

How do you research and analyze industry trends?

Researching and analyzing industry trends helps you understand what is happening in your business market that could impact your new business. For example, if you are starting a sandwich shop, you might want to find out what the most popular sandwiches in your area are, as well as people's preferred bread, toppings and sides. You will also want to know if rent is high right now, if a lot of new sandwich shops have recently opened, or if there are issues with having the supplies you need delivered.

Your industry research will help you identify trends over time that you'll want to analyze for impact to your business. These could include negative or positive impacts (areas of growth and opportunity!).

There are a few steps you should take to start this research:

1. Write down aspects of your industry you want to research. What topics or areas might impact your business?
2. Start with an online search. Keep your searches focused on one topic or focus area at a time.
3. If you're good with building slides or spreadsheets, use those tools to document your learnings.
4. Document your sources. Copy and paste the URL or entity you're using for your information so you can find it again in the future.
5. Use the data and information you've collected to list 3–5 market trends that could impact your business.

Workshop Session

Before you start your trends research, take the time to think about what trends you already follow. They could be sports trends, shopping or beauty trends, business trends or whatever interests you. Trends are everywhere. What makes the trends you follow interesting to you? How can you replicate this with your trends analysis?

I've learned that people will forget what you said, people will forget what you did, but people will never forget how you made them feel.

Maya Angelou

Industry Trends – Research

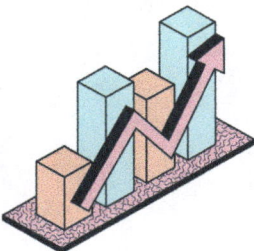

Your Industry Trends

1.

2.

3.

4.

5.

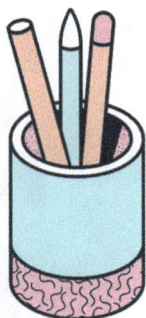

How do you create and activate an advertising plan?

An advertising plan is your roadmap for letting your target market know you exist. While the ideal situation is that you create amazing, viral social media content so everyone knows who you are and what you offer, the reality is often quite different. An advertising plan often requires investing in paid media promotion.

So what is advertising? It's using the information you collected on your target market—what media (news, websites, social media platforms, streaming, etc.) your customers use, what motivates them, who are they—to create a plan to reach the market with your message and create awareness!

This overview will give you some insight into advertising, but we recommend you hire or consult with a professional if you're unfamiliar with advertising concepts. That way, you're sure to invest your money and time wisely.

We cover three main concepts as part of this plan, including both paid and unpaid or organic forms of outreach.

1. Online and Offline Paid Channels – What advertising does your target market use or see or read?
2. Email Marketing – Does it make sense to use email? How can you start email marketing?
3. Social Media Strategy – What platforms should you use? What is the difference between paid vs. organic? How do you create content strategy and set up a post calendar?

Unplug and Take a Break

Advertising can be fun, but only if you're enjoying it! Take a break and collect your thoughts before you start on the next section. Think about your favorite things and what makes you laugh. Then, tackle this section!

Keep on going, and the chances are that you will stumble on something, perhaps when you are least expecting it. I never heard of anyone ever stumbling on something sitting down.

Charles F. Kettering

Online and Offline Paid Channels

Remember the list of media you created for your target market? Grab that list! Use it for your channels and outreach below:

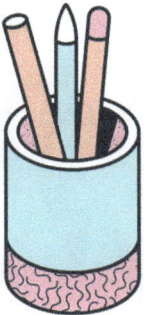

Example: Your consumer is between ages 18–24. They play video games, love dogs and are finding their way into world through college and work. They interact with TikTok, Discord, and go to their local coffee shop (bulletin boards!) and dog park (online sites for dog owners). Your marketing channels would be: TikTok (social and ads), Discord ads and interactions, video game websites (Twitch, etc.) and dog lovers' sites (Petco, blogs, etc.), the local coffee shop bulletin board, and college boards. What else can you think of? 112

Online Paid Channels

As you continue planning, it's easier to break out paid media into online and offline channels. Online refers to advertising with a digital or online component - like websites, e-commerce sites, advertising via mobile apps, etc. List your Online Paid Channels below.

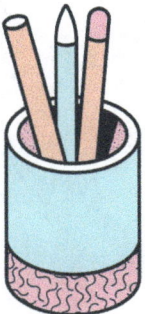

Offline Paid Channels

Offline channels refer to paid media that is not online, so this refers to newspaper ads, magazine ads, billboards, events and more. Have some fun with all of the options! List your Offline Paid Channels below.

Email Marketing

Does it make sense for you to start your own email marketing? How often would you send emails (quarterly, monthly, weekly)? What messages would your target market want to receive? What kind of creative or content would the target market want to read about?

Hint: Look for easy email templates from online companies! A quick Google search for email marketing will turn up a few options for easy-start guides and companies you can work with.

Email Marketing

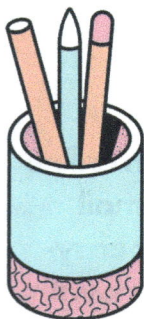

Social Media Strategy

Social media plays a vital role in many business marketing strategies and could easily take up this entire book! We'll focus on the basics, assuming that you already know how to post, create content and interact.

Let's start with what platforms you'll use (e.g., TikTok, Instagram, Facebook, Twitter) and why those platforms are important for your business. (Hint: Consider your target market!)

Next, we'll take your list and create a content strategy for each platform based on the creative needs of each. Considering your business, what messages do you want to convey, and what kinds of images fit your business?

Next, you'll consider how you want to invest in organic or unpaid social media and how you want to invest in paid social media, such as promoted posts or offers.

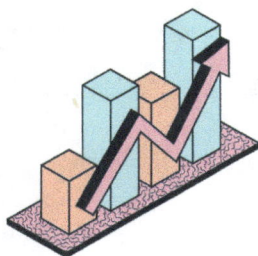

Finally, you'll set a calendar of posts, which will help you stay consistent and think ahead to special events, for which you'll want to create special posts or images. Remember to create social accounts specific to your business! It's a good idea to separate business and personal here.

Social Media Platforms

List your platforms and why each platform is good for your business.

Platform:

Why you want to use it:

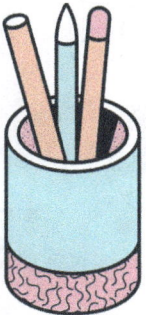

Platform:

Why you want to use it:

Social Media Platforms

List your platforms and why each platform is good for your business.

Platform:

Why you want to use it:

Platform:

Why you want to use it:

Social Media Platforms

List your platforms and why each platform is good for your business.

Platform:

Why you want to use it:

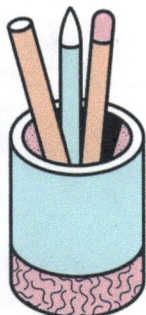

Platform:

Why you want to use it:

Social Media Content Strategy

List your platforms below, then list the kinds of content you'll need for each (e.g., TikTok needs short videos) and what messages you want to use.

Platform:

Content Types:

Messages:

Platform:

Content Types:

Messages:

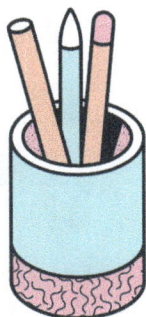

Social Media Content Strategy

Platform:

Content Types:

Messages:

Platform:

Content Types:

Messages:

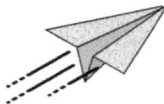

Social Media Content Strategy

Platform:

Content Types:

Messages:

Platform:

Content Types:

Messages:

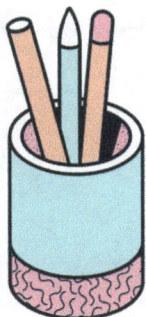

Paid vs. Organic Social Media

Organic content is posts you create and share for free on a platform. Paid social posts are just that: content you promote or pay to post to people outside of your followers because you believe this content will drive more interested audiences to your business. It's best to craft a plan for what you want to pay to promote and determine your budget. Use these next few pages to get started.

Platform:

Monthly budget:

Paid content:

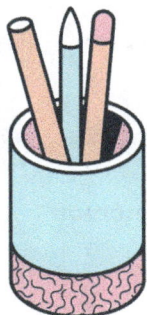

Friendly Feedback

Social media is a big undertaking, and it's important to have a plan for success. Part of that success is being sure to impart your specific knowledge. Your trusted colleagues can often help you uncover your niche and your style. Record their ideas here:

Knowledge exists to be imparted.

Ralph Waldo Emerson

Paid vs. Organic Social Media

Platform:

Monthly Budget:

Paid Content:

Platform:

Monthly Budget:

Paid Content:

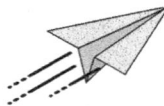

Paid vs. Organic Social Media

Platform:

Monthly Budget:

Paid Content:

Platform:

Monthly Budget:

Paid Content:

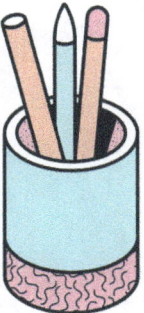

Paid vs. Organic Social Media

Platform:

Monthly Budget:

Paid Content:

Platform:

Monthly Budget:

Paid Content:

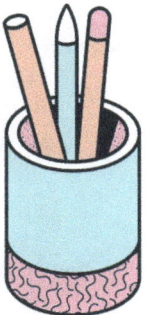

Social Media Post Calendar

A post calendar will help you stay consistent with your posts, which will keep your audience engaged and give you more opportunities for growth. This template will help you plan high-level posts and times during the day you want to post.

You can create an editable version of this calendar using Google Sheets or another platform, so you can update your post topics for special occasions or messages you want to share.

Platform, Day of Week, Time of Day

Platform:

	Morning	Afternoon	Evening
MON			

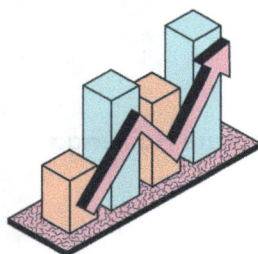

Research what kinds of posts you want to share on which days (e.g., Mondays are for motivational quotes). Each day can use a standard theme, or you can post using the latest news and information. Also, research and create a monthly events and celebrations calendar so you can post special messages during holidays or events.

Workshop Session

Stop and research! Spend some time online with your favorite social media accounts. Notice what kinds of themes they use and what events they celebrate. There are calendars of events for every day of the year—choose the events you want to celebrate with your business and determine why they might be relevant for your audiences. You might also want to take the time to create a quote and image library you can use for future reference.

> Some people dream of success, while other people get up every morning and make it happen.
>
> **Wayne Huizenga**

Social Media Post Calendar

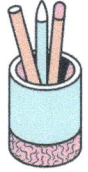

Platform:

	Morning	Afternoon	Evening
MON			
TUE			
WED			
THU			
FRI			
SAT			
SUN			

Social Media Post Calendar

Platform:

	Morning	Afternoon	Evening
MON			
TUE			
WED			
THU			
FRI			
SAT			
SUN			

Social Media Post Calendar

Platform:

	Morning	Afternoon	Evening
MON			
TUE			
WED			
THU			
FRI			
SAT			
SUN			

Social Media Post Calendar

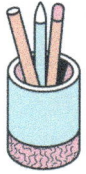

Platform:

	Morning	Afternoon	Evening
MON			
TUE			
WED			
THU			
FRI			
SAT			
SUN			

Social Media Post Calendar

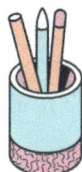

Platform:

	Morning	Afternoon	Evening
MON			
TUE			
WED			
THU			
FRI			
SAT			
SUN			

Social Media Post Calendar

Platform:

	Morning	Afternoon	Evening
MON			
TUE			
WED			
THU			
FRI			
SAT			
SUN			

Social Media Post Calendar

Platform:

	Morning	Afternoon	Evening
MON			
TUE			
WED			
THU			
FRI			
SAT			
SUN			

Social Media Post Calendar

Platform:

	Morning	Afternoon	Evening
MON			
TUE			
WED			
THU			
FRI			
SAT			
SUN			

Why should you consider public relations?

A brief public relations overview is included here because it can be a valuable asset for a well-rounded marketing plan.

Public relations, or PR, refers to sharing your business news, such as a launch or new opening, with a news publication or relevant blogger with the intent to have this information published for free as a story on the publication's site or in their printed newsletter.

This is a crowded marketplace, and most publications only want to publish information that is truly newsworthy —something their readers will find useful or interesting.

You'll also want to think about crafting stories focused on what your consumers will want to hear and find useful— this is not the time for a sales pitch! This PR plan will help you get started, but consult a professional if you want to do more with this!

There are three things to consider when you think about PR:
- What magazines, blogs, news outlets or other publications (offline and online) will be most interested in big news from your business?
- What messaging will matter most to the publication you want to publish your news?
- How will you reach out to people at the publication? Do you know anyone who works there? Can you find a contact or submission option online?

Unplug and Take a Break

Public relations taps into your extroverted side, even for those who don't have an extroverted side! As this requires outreach and bravery, it's a good time to take a few minutes and center yourself. Find what makes you happy and prepare for these next steps. Remember, there are people who want to hear your story—you just need to find them and build your tribe of people.

If you don't give up, you still have a chance. Giving up is the greatest failure.

Mark Cuban

Publications Related to Your Business

Publication:

Publication Website:

Publication Theme or Relevant Information:

Relevant Message or News to Send:

Outreach Email:

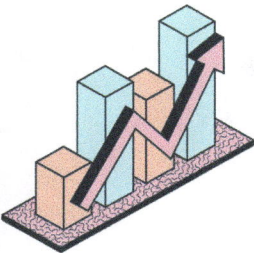

Publications Related to Your Business

Publication:

Publication Website:

Publication Theme or Relevant Information:

Relevant Message or News to Send:

Outreach Email:

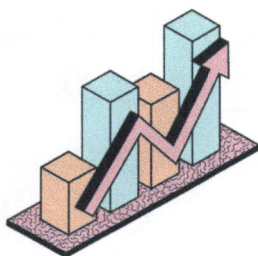

Publications Related to Your Business

Publication:

Publication Website:

Publication Theme or Relevant Information:

Relevant Message or News to Send:

Outreach Email:

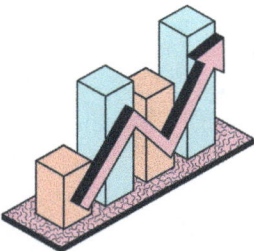

Publications Related to Your Business

Publication:

Publication Website:

Publication Theme or Relevant Information:

Relevant Message or News to Send:

Outreach Email:

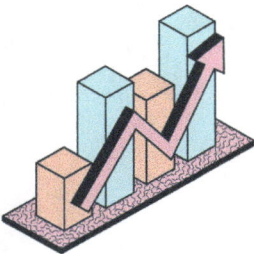

Publications Related to Your Business

Publication:

Publication Website:

Publication Theme or Relevant Information:

Relevant Message or News to Send:

Outreach Email:

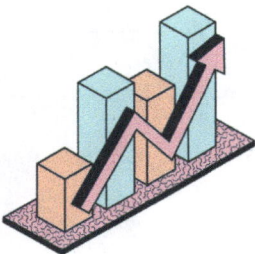

Publications Related to Your Business

Publication:

Publication Website:

Publication Theme or Relevant Information:

Relevant Message or News to Send:

Outreach Email:

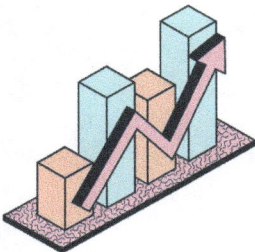

Publications Related to Your Business

Publication:

Publication Website:

Publication Theme or Relevant Information:

Relevant Message or News to Send:

Outreach Email:

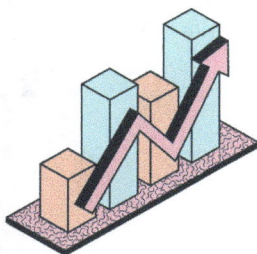

Publications Related to Your Business

Publication:

Publication Website:

Publication Theme or Relevant Information:

Relevant Message or News to Send:

Outreach Email:

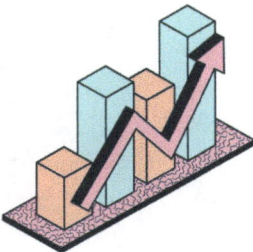

Publications Related to Your Business

Publication:

Publication Website:

Publication Theme or Relevant Information:

Relevant Message or News to Send:

Outreach Email:

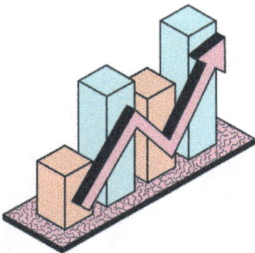

Publications Related to Your Business

Publication:

Publication Website:

Publication Theme or Relevant Information:

Relevant Message or News to Send:

Outreach Email:

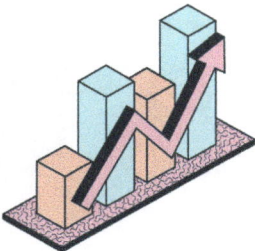

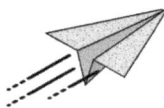

Operations Plan

Operations are crucial for defining how your business will reach its goals. The operations plan defines the day-to-day steps you'll need to take to get your product or service to market, how to handle sales, what inputs you need to consider and how you'll make money.

This mapping can include digital or physical space you need to be successful. Keep in mind, not every plan includes physical space—you may only need a website!

An operations plan includes the following:

- Defining where you'll sell (online or offline) – you'll need to consider what kind of website you need and if you'll need a physical space in which to sell or store products. Don't forget physical space for product storage!

- Product or Service Pricing – You've learned a lot about competitive pricing, so use this as a beginning reference. What do you need to charge, and how much do you need to sell to be profitable?
- Sales Strategy – How do you plan to sell? What messages matter? Do you need sales staff? What about pricing for advertising?
- Customer Service – How will you handle reviews or customer needs?

Selling Your Product or Service Online? Offline?

It's best to draw pics here! Do some research on your online needs—website, social outreach, e-commerce! And your offline needs—do you need a storefront, storage space or shipping?

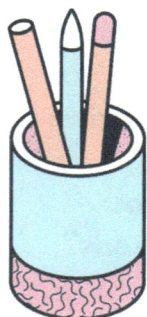

You can start to map our your costs here! Everything you've done so far has a cost to it, from social media, advertising planning, public relations, and now a website or storefront. Knowing the costs of items will help you with pricing and with funding for your business.

How much will you charge? How much do you need to sell to break even? Make money?

What are your services or products worth to consumers? (Hint - what are your competitors charging?)

While you're researching, how do you compare to the competition for product features or services?

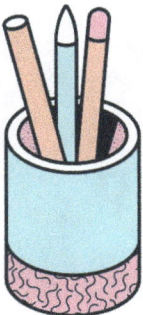

**How much have you invested so far, and what will you ne[ed]
to break even or make money? How much more do you
need to invest?**

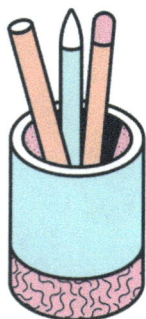

Sales Strategy

How will you sell your product or service?

How will you reach your customers?

Sales Strategy Continued

Will you hire a salesperson? How does this role fit in your staff plan?

What does outreach look like for your business?

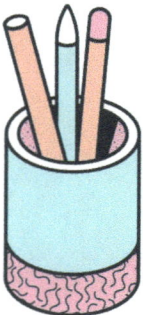

Customer Service Approach

You've built a great product or service! You've started to sell and your customers have questions—or worse, someone leaves a bad review. How do you handle customer service and reviews?

How can you use AI, such as a Chatbot to help?

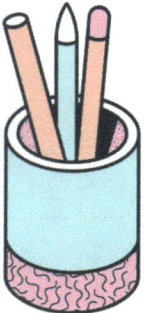

Customer Service Continued

Do you need to hire a service or additional staff to handle customer service questions?

What is in your Frequently Asked Questions (FAQ) section?

Branding Strategy

When you think about a company, you're typically thinking about the visual aspects of the company—from logos to colors, fonts and overall mood. It's this branding portion of a company that conveys emotion. Using visual elements, what do you want a consumer to think about you? What is the "business face" you want to show to the world?

Keep a few things in mind as you work through this section. Consistency is important (there is a reason you recognize logos). Colors and fonts convey emotion and meaning.

Branding strategy includes the following:

- Start with your meaning – When someone sees your logo, font and colors, what do you want them to think about your business?
- Colors – What colors do you want for your business? What do those colors say about your business?
- Fonts – How should you choose fonts to represent your business? Are the fonts you choose representative of your brand?
- Logo – How do you choose a logo designer? What are the easy ways to have a logo designed?

Unplug and Take a Break

You've made it so far! Branding is critical to a successful business, and it requires clear and consistent thought. Before you start this next section, take the time to consider your favorite things. What do they say to you, what colors are you drawn to, and what images and visual aspects of artwork, advertisements, and more appeal to you? Your brand will be what you live and breathe in your business, so make this a fun and enjoyable process.

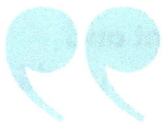

Your brand has to come together at every touchpoint.

Jonathan Bottomley

Define Your Business in 5 Adjectives:

What do you want people to think about your business? In this next section, you'll ideate a series of adjectives that could describe your business. Let your mind wander, and add all the descriptors that come to mind. After you've added all the possibilities, you'll narrow them down to five that you want to use to define your business.

These five adjectives will help you stay focused as you choose brand colors and logo design. They'll even help you develop communications and outreach. Branding isn't just about colors or design; branding is how you want the world to view your company.

Use the resources listed below to help ideate your potential adjectives. If you get stuck, think about your favorite brands or your competition—what adjectives come to mind when you look at what they've built?

Resources:
Lists of Adjectives – https://simplicable.com/en/words-to-describe-business
Synonym Generator – https://www.synonym.com/

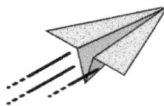

Giant List of Adjectives

Don't overthink it! Write out all the adjectives that come to mind when you think about your business.

Your Adjective Choices

Now filter your choices down to a list of 7–12 adjectives that you want to people to know about your business. Where do you want to focus?

Your Final 5 Adjectives

Make your final cut. Include your rationale for why you chose these adjectives and how they differentiate your business.

1.

2.

3.

4.

5.

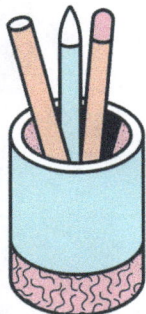

Color Meanings and Fonts

Now that you've aligned on key adjectives to describe your business, we can use those words as themes to choose your business colors and fonts.

Some businesses can take color and font risks because it is part of the overall brand meaning. Other businesses might choose more traditional colors and fonts because they want to be more conservative in their messaging. Regardless of your choice, colors and fonts are important visual aspects of your business, so take the time to determine what you want to say to your customers and clients.

Once you've selected your colors and fonts using the exercises from the following pages, you'll want to consistently use the colors and fonts across your logo, websites, printed materials and more. Consistent use will ensure customers see your colors, fonts and logo so they will recall your business. Think about businesses like McDonald's or Walmart—you likely know what these colors, fonts and logos look like. Consistency will help your business achieve similar (though likely smaller scale!) recollection with your customers.

As you get started on this next section, stop and research first. What brands are around you? What brands do you love? What brands do you hate? What colors remind you of certain brands?

The more you think about the brands around you and the more you research, the more you'll find just how impactful a brand's colors and fonts can be in how you perceive those companies.

Where do you put the fear when you choose to innovate? The fear is there, but you have to find a place to put it.

Seth Godin

What Colors Mean

Black — Sophisticated, Formal, Stylish, Authoritative

Red — Passion, Boldness, Aggression, Strength

Green — Trustworthy, Wealth, Natural, Harmony

Orange — Happy, Energetic, Friendly

Blue — Honest, Conservative, Dependable

Yellow — Optimistic, Trustworthy, Smart, Confident

Purple — Majestic, Mysterious, Creative

White — Purity, Cleanliness, Youthful

- While the above primary color palette describes what these colors convey, you can choose any shade or any color that works for your business.
- The psychology of colors in logos can help to drive your brand strategy and how people perceive your business.
- Whatever colors you choose, be sure to document them with precision so you can use the same colors consistently in your logo, marketing, and business outreach efforts.

Friendly Feedback

Your brand is how you present your business to the world. A good first step is to collect thoughts from trusted colleagues and friends. Remember, thoughts and opinions aren't orders, but suggestions for you on your journey. Record important thoughts here:

Alone we can do so little; together we can do so much.

Helen Keller

Your List of Colors

Grab some colored pencils, crayons or markers and sketch out what colors you like, how they look together and what they say about your business.

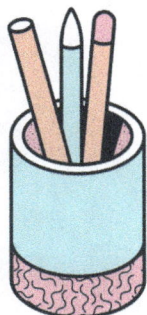

Final Colors

Choose 1–3 colors for your final list and show them below. Identify your primary colors and secondary or support colors and how to use them, along with the closest computer code colors for them. (https://htmlcolorcodes.com)

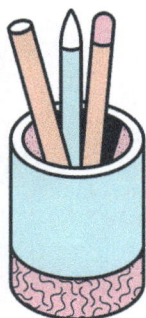

What Fonts Mean

Fonts have their own personality, and each font conveys a specific meaning based on its look and feel. Make sure your font says the right thing about your business and matches the tone of your adjectives and color choices.

Serif Fonts
traditional, reliable, sophisticated, formal

Sans Serif Fonts
modern, clean, objective, stable

Script Fonts
elegant, creative, familiar, stylish

DISPLAY & SPECIALTY FONTS
FUN, FRIENDLY, AMUSING, UNIQUE, EXPRESSIVE

- **Things to consider when choosing a font:**
  - **Choose a font fits your brand meaning and your color choices.**
  - **Avoid confusing or hard-to-read fonts.**
  - **Choose a font you can easily display on your website and other marketing efforts.**
- **Font inspiration can be found at the below sites:**
  - **https://fonts.google.com**
  - **https://fontjoy.com**

Your List of Fonts

List out the fonts you like and describe how you think they best fit your business brand strategy. Choose a primary font that you'll use in headlines and potentially in your logo and a secondary, easy-to-read font for your regular text.

Final Fonts

List your final fonts below. Identify your primary font and secondary or long-form text font, and describe how to use them.

Primary Font:

How will it be used?

Secondary Font:

How will it be used?

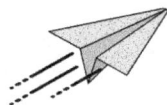

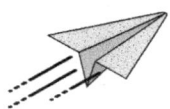

Logo Needs –
How to find a design(er)

You've done the work to understand your business brand, from descriptors to colors and fonts, all of which convey specific meanings about your brand and business.

Now you need a logo!

Your logo can be designed by a real person you work with to create a unique logo, or you can use a pre-existing design from a platform like Canva.

When using a logo designer, you might pay anywhere from a few dollars upwards of thousands, depending on how much time and effort you want to spend on your logo.

For now, it might be best to choose one of the resources below and either find a logo designer with styles similar to what you want, or go to a platform with hundreds of pre-existing templates you can use to design your own.

Just remember to be consistent with your colors and fonts.

Find a logo designer online –
https://www.fiverr.com

Use a pre-existing template and design your own logo –
https://www.canva.com

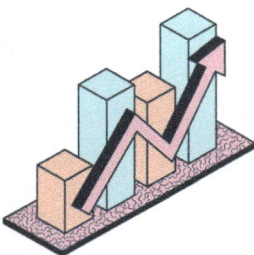

Your Branding Recap

Recap your brand work on this page and use it as a reference to stay consistent with your marketing and business design efforts.

Five Adjectives to Describe Your Business

1.
2.
3.
4.
5.

**Your Primary and Secondary Colors
(Pro Tip: Add the color codes below the boxes)**

☐ ☐ ☐ ☐ ☐

_____

_____

**Your Primary and Secondary Fonts
(Pro Tip: List how and when you'll use each)**

_____

_____

_____

_____

Sketch Your Logo Below

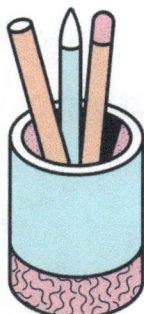

Executive Summary (Again)

In this section, you'll flip back to your original executive summary work and rewrite key elements using the information you've learned from completing the exercises and research in this book. Refine your statements as you write them again.

- **Brief Description of Your Product or Service**
  - **1–2 sentences clearly describing your offering**
- **Statement of Marketplace Need**
  - **1–2 sentences stating the problem you see in the market**
- **How Your Business Solves the Marketplace Need**
  - **A few short sentences on how your product or service solves the problem you see in the marketplace, including the benefit to your customers**
- **Unique Selling Proposition**
  - **How are you different from your competitors? What makes your business solution the best for the marketplace need?**

- **Mission Statement**
  - **Why do you exist? What is your overall goal and purpose?**
- **Business Values**
  - **Beliefs, philosophies, and principles that drive your business, what matters to your business, and how you present to your customers**
- **Business Vision**
  - **Where your company will be in the future. Align this to your business mission, goals and values**

Updated Executive Summary

Brief Description of Your Product or Service

Statement of Marketplace Need

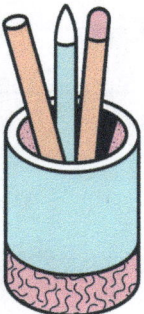

Updated Executive Summary

How Your Business Solves the Marketplace Need for Customers or Clients

Unique Selling Proposition

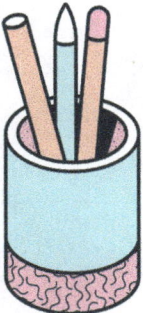

Updated Executive Summary

Mission Statement

Business Values

Business Vision

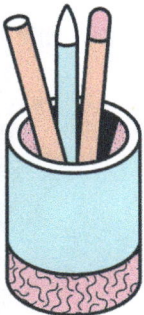

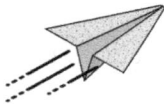

Write It Again –
Updated Executive Pitch

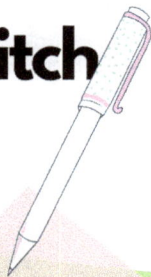

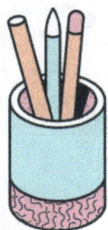

Stop Dreaming
Start Doing

Steps to Launch

You've built a good foundation! Now what is left for you to launch your business?

1. _____

2. _____

3. _____

4. _____

5. _____

6. _____

7. _____

8. _____

Opportunities don't happen. You create them.

Chris Grosser

Business Name & Website

This section is meant to remind you that the launch strategy often includes researching your business name and available websites.

While not every business needs a website, it's a good idea to have a landing page, at least, so when people search for your business online, you have a better chance of showing up in the search results.

There are many places to register a website and resources to help you build a website (http://www.fiverr.com is a great place to find help with this), which has made this task easier.

Resources

Research Site Names, Register Domains, Build Websites –
http://www.godaddy.com
http://www.wordpress.com
https://www.squarespace.com
https://www.wix.com

If you don't have a business name, it's a great idea to reach out to supportive friends and colleagues for their thoughts and advice!

Keep Going!!

Winning is great, sure, but if you are really going to do something in life, the secret is learning how to lose. Nobody goes undefeated all the time. If you can pick up after a crushing defeat, and go on to win again, you are going to be a champion someday.

Wilma Rudolph

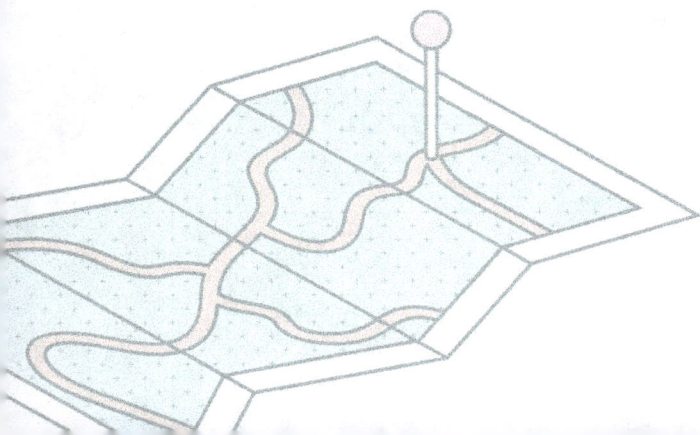

REMINDERS
FOR HARD DAYS

YOU ARE AN AMAZING HUMAN

THIS PHASE WILL PASS

YOU CAN ALWAYS START OVER

EVERYTHING WILL BE FINE

YOU ARE DOING YOUR BEST

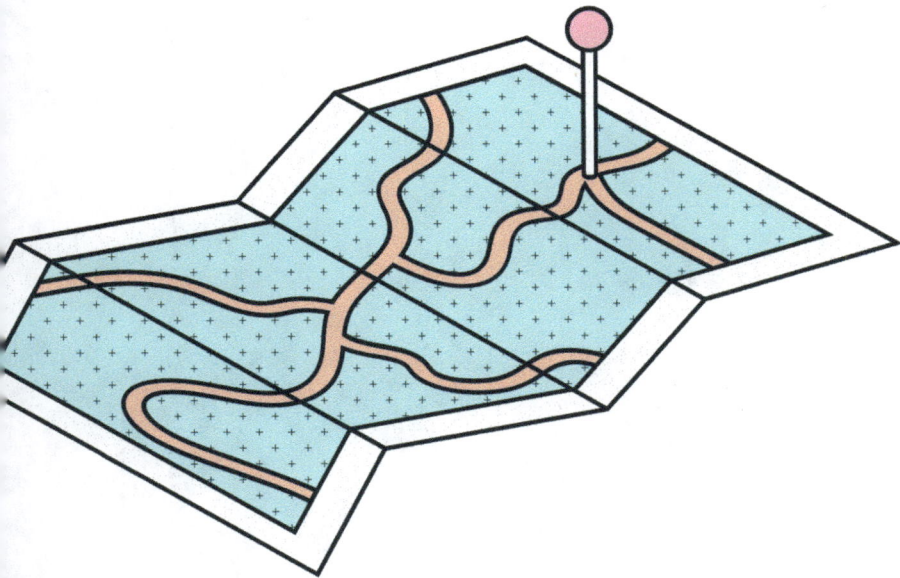

Your Roadmap to Success